BiG NATE

In the Zone

Lincoln Peirce

HarperCollins *Children's Books*

For the cousins

CHAPTER 1

A frozen waffle has ruined my life.

TEDDY'S frozen waffle, if you really want to know.
This whole disaster is totally his fault.

Teddy's one of my two best friends (Francis is the other), but I'm pretty ticked off at him right now. He's the reason I'm standing here in front of half the school, getting my butt handed to me by Principal Nichols.

It started yesterday in social studies. That's when Mrs Godfrey, aka Jabba the Gut, assigned a research paper. Guess who has to write about the War of 1812? Worst. Topic. EVER.

Inspired by those heartwarming words, I flipped through the textbook. And you know what it said about the War of 1812? Absolutely NOTHING. It was probably written in 1811. Anyway, that's when Teddy came to the rescue. . .

Sounded like a plan. After school, we ALL walked over to Teddy's:

Me. . .   Dee Dee. . .

          Francis. . .   and Chad.

And it went GREAT. Mr Ortiz's books were so full of boring facts and useless information – the kind of stuff teachers LOVE – that in no time at all, I pulled together a pretty rockin' outline.

So far, so good, right? Well, not quite. Because

late – like "I'm already in my jammies" later –
I was going through my backpack. . . and THE
OUTLINE WASN'T THERE!!

So I DIDN'T worry about it. I went to bed thinking my outline was safe in Teddy's kitchen. Little
did I know what would happen the next morning.

Ok, it probably didn't go EXACTLY like that. Whatever. The point was: When I got to school this morning, I found out that Teddy had turned my outline into a soggy, syrupy pile of confetti.

Sure, I could tell Mrs Godfrey the whole story. She LOVES listening to excuses. She's so UNDERSTANDING.

Class was starting in three minutes, and I had no outline. Talk about a stress fest. I was twitching like a bag of microwave popcorn. So I did what I always do when I get nervous.

I bonked myself on the head with an empty plastic bottle.

Yeah, maybe it's a little weird. But have you ever TRIED it? It feels good. It's relaxing. And it makes kind of a cool sound.

"What on EARTH are you doing?"

What was I doing? Wondering how the Bride of Sasquatch could have snuck up behind me, that's what. I mean, she's big, she's loud, and she smells like onions. How does she sneak up on ANYBODY?

What could I say? I was busted. I waited until she'd gone back into her classroom. Then I spotted the recycling bin over by the computer lab.

We now interrupt this flashback with a fact about plastic bottles: They're bouncy. That's what makes 'em such good stress busters. But it means that if you throw one, the chances are better than average that it's going to bounce off where you WANT it to go. . .

. . .and end up someplace ELSE. . .

. . .like THAT. Bull's-eye.

There. Now you know why the principal is yelling at me till his tonsils burst. That's the end of the flashback. . .

...AND THE **START** OF ANOTHER **FANTASTIC** DAY!

Note the sarcasm. I don't want to sound all whiny and everything, but my life STINKS lately.

It's not just one thing; it's a whole bunch of stuff.
And it all adds up to a hot, steaming pile of...

"I don't want to hear it," she says flatly. "Your 'funny stories' are usually total FICTION."

Before I can answer, Teddy's beside me.

HA! Hear THAT, lady? Teddy's backing me up! What do you say NOW?

If you're keeping score, that's Godfrey one, truth zero. I guess when you're a teacher, you don't sweat the small stuff. Like THE FACTS.

HAND IN AN OUTLINE BY THE END OF THE DAY, NATE, AND YOU COULD STILL EARN **HALF CREDIT!**

THAT SOUNDS ABOUT RIGHT!

HALF CREDIT FOR A **HALF-WIT!**

Ugh. Here's ANOTHER reason my life's a total bitefest lately. Gina's been even more obnoxious than usual. See that smile on her face? She

LOVES to see me get in trouble. It's like Christmas for her. And right now, every day's a holiday.

Gina smirks. "That's not even ORIGINAL," she hisses. "You used the exact same insult on me YESTERDAY!"

I feel my cheeks start to burn. I DID, didn't I? I'm reusing MY OWN MATERIAL. Wow, even my trash-talking has gone stale. I can't do ANYTHING right.

WHAT A **SLUMP** I'M IN!

Actually, "slump" might not be the word I'm looking for. Slumps usually happen in SPORTS – like when the game just doesn't go your way, no matter how hard you try. I've been in sports slumps before, and it's usually not that big a deal. Unless you have a psycho for a coach.

No, this is more than a slump. It's bad luck, that's what it is. HORRIBLE luck. And I can't find a way out of it.

The bell finally rings, and the gang joins me as we all file out of the classroom.

He looks so serious, I can't help but crack a smile. It's impossible to stay mad at Teddy.

"It wasn't your fault," I tell him. "You TRIED to take the blame!"

"Is she ever NOT in full rage mode?" Francis asks.

"Good point," the rest of us say together.

"I can't," I groan. "I've got to get that stupid outline done." I shuffle off towards the library. War of 1812, here I come.

"You keep your chin up, Nate!" Dee Dee chirps as I trudge down the hallway. "The day's just starting! It'll get better!"

"It HAS to," I call back.

CHAPTER 2

"Nate! Just the kiddo I'm looking for!" Mrs Hickson greets me as I step into the library.

I feel like telling her NOTHING'S right up my alley these days. The way my luck's going, if I ended up in an alley. . .

...I'D PROBABLY GET **MUGGED!**

"Uh. . . thanks, but I'll have to look at them later," I say. "I've got to do some social studies first."

"REALLY?" Her eyebrows practically pop off her face. "Well, by all means, Nate, go right ahead!"

Nice. Does she have to look so SHOCKED? I may not be Joe Scholar, but it isn't like I NEVER come in here to do classwork. It only SEEMS that way.

FAVOURITE LIBRARY *ACTIVITIES!*

1. TABLE FOOTBALL

Kickin' off!

FLIK!

PLUNK!

OW!

"Do you have any stuff I could look at about the War of 1812?" I ask (as if I really care).

"I just might!" she answers. "Let me see what I can find!" She bustles off to who knows where.

MAYBE SHE'S CHECKING THE "BORING BOOKS THAT NOBODY WANTS TO READ" SECTION.

Anyway, looks like I'm here at the right time.

When Hickey's in a good mood – like now – she's actually pretty nice. But like all teachers, she definitely has a dark side. I've seen her get pretty mad. Not GODFREY mad, but she's on the chart.

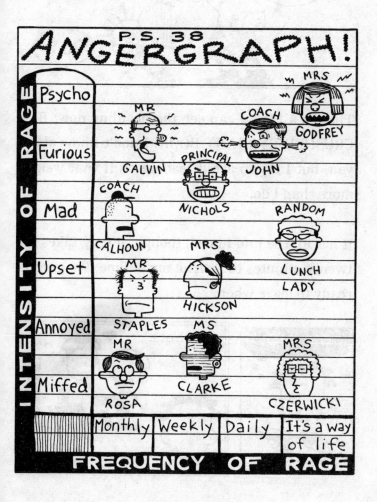

Now she's back with a book the size of a stack of lunch trays.

Thanks a LOT. I can see the headline now: BOY CRUSHED BY GIANT BOOK. I don't know about you, but I try to avoid reading stuff that weighs more than I do.

It has all the info I need, though. It only takes me twenty minutes to rewrite my outline. I'm getting ready to leave when. . .

Look at THIS, everybody – it's JENNY AND ARTUR, P.S. 38's most popular couple! Aren't they sweet? Aren't they adorable? Aren't they. . .

SICKENING?

Don't get me wrong. I'm not saying JENNY'S sickening. She's completely awesome. And I know a little something about awesomeness.

No, what grosses me out is seeing the two of them TOGETHER, slobbering all over each other like a pair of lovesick puppies. Okay, so they're a couple. Fine. Do they have to be so OBNOXIOUS about it?

Did she just call him "POOKIE BEAR"? Pardon my

gag reflex. Artur's no pookie bear. I can come up
with WAY better names for him than THAT. . .

...AND I WILL!

What Should She Call Him?

Oh, Artur, you're such a **INSERT NAME HERE!**

Yes! Is true!

- ♥ Fart Bucket
- ♥ Piece of Dry Toast
- ♥ Bogey Bunny
- ♥ Ingrown Toenail
- ♥ Cuddle Slug
- ♥ Glass of Warm Prune Juice
- ♥ Sweat Monkey
- ♥ Zitwagon
- ♥ Sad Little Clown
- ♥ Barf-o-matic
- ♥ Sand Crab
- ♥ Weasel Boy
- ♥ Nate Wanna-Be
- ♥ Pea Brain
- ♥ Wussykins
- ♥ Soon-to-be former boyfriend

You're probably reading this list and thinking I'm hating on Artur. But believe it or not, I actually kind of LIKE the guy. He just bugs me sometimes, that's all. AND he's Jenny's love puppet.

HI, NATE!

CHAD! I THOUGHT YOU WERE PLAYING ADD-ON IN THE CAFETORIUM!

"We were, but then some seventh graders started throwing tacos at us," he says.

CHAD FACT:
He's small for his age,
so his grandmother taught
him this saying:

"FIRST TO RIPEN, FIRST TO ROT!"

"Seventh graders are such a pain," I mutter.

Chad nods. "Tell me about it. My hair smells like guacamole now."

He pulls up a chair beside me. "What are you doing?"

"Ooh! Can I be in it?"

"Sure, why not?" I say. "It's always fun to invent new characters."

"What's so funny?" he asks, looking a little hurt.

"Chad, no offence, but. . . I don't think you're the super-villain type."

"I guess you're right," he admits. "Maybe I'm more of a 'loyal sidekick' kind of guy."

"Now THAT'S a good idea!" I tell him. "Ultra-Nate could USE a sidekick!" I start drawing.

THE *AMAZING* ADVENTURES OF
ULTRA - NATE!
SUPER 6TH GRADER
...and introducing his *DYNAMIC* new crime-fighting partner: **MEGA-CHAD!!**

Chad beams. "Mega-Chad! I LIKE that!"

HOW ABOUT GIVING ME A MASK?

"OK," I say, making a few pencil strokes. "Any other requests?"

Chad doesn't answer right away, and when I look up from the table, I can see that he's blushing.

CAN YOU PUT **HER** IN IT?

"Who, Maya?" I say, surprised.

Chad nods shyly, his cheeks now fire-engine red. "Maybe I could rescue her or save her life or something." Then, quickly, he adds, "In your comics, I mean."

Wow, THIS is news. I had no idea Chad had a thing for Maya.

"All right, trusty sidekick," I tell him, leaning over my notebook again. "I'll see what I can do."

"Wouldn't that be cool?" Chad says when he's done reading. "Having super powers like that?"

IMAGINE BEING ABLE TO **FLY!**

"We might not be able to fly, but we can do the next best thing," I tell him. "Follow me!"

We angle over to the Book Nook, where a bunch of giant beanbag chairs sit empty in the corner. I do a quick 360 to make sure there's no sign of Hickey. "Give me a hand, Chad," I whisper.

BOOK NOOK

READING ROCKS!

PILE THESE UP!

Chad looks baffled. "What are we doing?"

"Making a crash pad," I tell him.

"You're gonna JUMP?" he asks, his eyes widening.

"Superheroes don't jump, Chad," I remind him as I scramble up on to a table. "We FLY!"

He looks around anxiously. "But what if Mrs Hickson sees us?"

I bend my knees, ready to launch myself into the pile. "Chad, RELAX! Kids do this all the time and never get busted! Hickey's not going to suspect a thing!"

CHAPTER 3

Uh-oh. Can I take that back?

"You blew a HOLE in it!" Chad squeaks.

Yeah, a HUMONGOUS hole. The seam of one of the beanbags is split wide open, and. . .

Tiny Styrofoam pellets are pouring out on to the floor. This is a DISASTER.

"Quick, Chad!" I hiss, trying to shovel the pellets back through the hole. "We've got to clean this up before Hickey. . ."

She gives me the VSHE – the Very Scary Hairy Eyeball.

Then comes the audio.

"Loud noises are not WELCOME in the library, Nate," she growls.

...ESPECIALLY THE SOUND OF A BEANBAG CHAIR EXPLODING!

I guess I could point out that it didn't EXPLODE, technically. And that if she wants to keep it quiet in here, maybe she should stop SHRIEKING at me.

..BUT NOW'S PROBABLY NOT THE TIME.

AVE N IDEA W YOU TH YOU'RE DOING BUT IT COMPL UNA

After airing out her dentures for a couple of minutes, Hickey finally stops to breathe. She looks at the Styrofoam scattered all over the floor, then does one of those slo-mo librarian head shakes.

BEANBAG CHAIRS DON'T GROW ON **TREES**, BOYS!

They DON'T? Wow, thanks for the red-hot news flash. I'll add it to my list of. . .

AMAZING OBSERVATIONS ONLY **ADULTS** CAN MAKE!

I never **THOUGHT** of that!

These dishes aren't going to wash **THEMSELVES**, mister!

This is **GYM CLASS**, not a **PLEASURE CRUISE!**

OOLP!

CJ

From out of nowhere, she pulls a small pink pad.
Great. Another detention slip for my collection.
"You'll notice, Nate, that I'm signing this 'Mrs
Hickson,'" she tells me.

Chad looks terrified. I don't think he's ever been to detention. In fact, he's ALMOST a member of. . .

1. GINA HEMPHILL-TOMS
Yes, she **DID** get detention once (thank you, Ben Franklin), **BUT...**
THAT WILL *NEVER* HAPPEN AGAIN!! NEVERNEVER**NEVER** *NEVER!*

Hickey – I mean Mrs Hickson – points a finger at the leaky beanbag. "That needs to be fixed," she announces.

TAKE IT TO MS BRINDLE.

Chad instantly perks up. "Ms Brindle! YES!" he says under his breath.

I'll explain later why Chad is a major Ms Brindle groupie. Right now, though, we have to deal with these stupid pellets. Which turn out to have a MAJOR static cling problem.

Not to mention our hair, our faces. . . the stupid little things stick to EVERYTHING. In a couple of minutes, we both look like we've been swimming in an ocean of dandruff.

"Did you hear that?" Chad whispers excitedly.

SHE SAID I'M ADORABLE!!

Maybe Maya was just being nice, or maybe she really DOES think Chad's adorable. Either way, I'm happy for him. I feel sort of guilty that he got detention when all he did was—

NATE!

YOU LOOK LIKE A COMPLETE IDIOT!

"Wait a minute," I say to Chad after Jenny and Artur walk off. "How come I'm an IDIOT and you're ADORABLE?"

He shrugs happily. "Just lucky, I guess."

Lucky? I don't even know what that word MEANS any more. So far today, I've been hung out to dry by Godfrey, Nichols, and Hickson. I'm three for three.

WILL MS BRINDLE MAKE IT **FOUR?**

While Chad and I lug the beanbag chair to her classroom, I can tell you about Ms Brindle. She teaches "Life Skills," which isn't anything like a real class. It's more of a cross between

MS BRINDLE FACT:
Her classroom always smells like cinnamon.

MMMMMM!

SNIFF
SNIFF
SNUFF
SNUFF

a TV cooking show and a visit to your grandmother. There's no textbook and no homework. It's just Ms Brindle teaching us random stuff.

Some of it's lame. . .

. . .and some of it's awesome.

Anyway, here's the one thing you need to know about Ms Brindle: She's the nicest teacher in the whole school. So if SHE ends up yelling at me. . .

THAT'S why Chad's such a huge Ms Brindle fan. He's got a serious sweet tooth, and he knows that whenever he walks into her room, she's going to offer him cookies or brownies or. . .

Chad's face falls flatter than a mashed cat. "C-cabbage?" he stammers.

YOU DON'T HAVE...UM... ANYTHING ELSE?

"I'm afraid not. Sorry, Chad," Ms Brindle says with a smile.

IT'S PART OF THE SCHOOL'S NEW "FITNESS ZONE" PROGRAMME!

WHAT'S "FITNESS ZONE"?

MUNCH MUNCH OOLP!

"Principal Nichols will explain it at the assembly tomorrow," she continues. "For MY class, it means that from now on, we'll be focusing on making healthy food choices."

"Oh," Chad says, looking like he knows that "healthy food choices" is actually code for "stuff you wouldn't even feed your pet gerbil."

Then Ms Brindle nods towards the rip in the beanbag chair. "Oh, my goodness," she says.

"By diving off a table," Chad adds. Uh, Earth to Chad: Ever hear the phrase "TOO MUCH INFORMATION"?

But Ms Brindle doesn't miss a beat. She just winks and says, "Sounds like the two of you could use a SEWING lesson!"

She shows us how to thread a needle, sew up the seam, and hide the stitches. In no time flat, our beanbag's as good as new. Now that's TEACHING.

"Good ol' Ms Brindle," I say, after Chad and I leave her room and turn the corner.

"I was trying to be polite," he says. "But now my mouth tastes like I just gargled with coleslaw."

I glance at the clock by the stairwell. "We've still got ten minutes before English."

IF WE HUSTLE THIS THING BACK TO THE LIBRARY, WE'LL HAVE TIME TO GRAB A QUICK SNACK!

OOH! YAY!

After Hickey gives the mended beanbag a nod of approval, we double back to the cafetorium to hit the vending machine.

THE SNACKS ARE ON ME, CHAD!

DRIUM

! !

S N A C K S

We stand there for a minute like we're paralysed.
Then Chad finally says something. Sort of.

"This must be part of that new 'Fitness Zone' thing," I say grimly.

THEY'RE REPLACING ALL THE SNACKS WITH **BIRD FOOD!**

"I. . . uh. . . I don't think I'm all that hungry any more," Chad mumbles.

Yeah, I'm feeling a little sick myself. No more candy bars. No more gummi treats. And – I'll try to say this without freaking out – NO MORE CHEEZ DOODLES! Goodbye, bad. Hello, worse.

I DON'T KNOW HOW MUCH MORE OF THIS I CAN **TAKE!**

NATE!

I turn to see Dee Dee hurrying towards us.

She's out of breath. "THERE you are!" she gasps. "I've been looking all OVER for you!"

"How come?"

"To give you a message!"

PRINCIPAL NICHOLS WANTS TO SEE YOU IN HIS OFFICE!

NOW!

CHAPTER 4

What did I do THIS time? Principal Nichols already made me his punching bag ONCE today. Is he going to bawl me out AGAIN. . .

...JUST FOR FUN?

WELL, HELLO THERE, NATE!

"Hi, Mrs Shipulski," I say. She's the school secretary. If there's any upside to visiting the principal's office, she's it. Here's why:

Wait a minute. Speaking of jelly beans...

WHERE **ARE** THEY?

Mrs Shipulski reads my mind. "No more jelly beans, Nate," she says. "We're becoming a candy-free office."

INSTEAD, HOW ABOUT SOME DELICIOUS **WASABI PEAS**?

UHHHH...

AH, **NATE**! LONG TIME, NO SEE! HA HA!

COME IN!

Phew. Saved by the Big Fella himself. No offence to Mrs Shipulski, but those peas look like a bowl full of rabbit droppings.

"Nate," Principal Nichols says as he shuts the door behind us. "You may have noticed a few CHANGES around the school."

Yeah, like the vending machine turning into a salad bar. But, hey, he's not SHOUTING at me. Guess he's moved past that little plastic bottle incident.

"I was planning to make an announcement about those very changes at tomorrow's assembly," he continues.

THEN... I HAD AN IDEA!

✳CHUCKLE!✳ WELL, THERE'S A FIRST TIME FOR EVERYTHING!

WHY NOT LIVEN THINGS UP WITH A LITTLE MUSIC?

Music? Where's he going with this? And why's he telling ME about it?

"You belong to a BAND, don't you, Nate?"

"CAPTURE THE CRUSTACEAN," OR "BOIL THE LOBSTER," OR...?

ENSLAVE THE MOLLUSK!

Yeah, and FYI: I don't just BELONG to the greatest sixth-grade rock band of all time. I STARTED it.

NATE'S *REAL-LIFE* COMIX presents...

BIRTH OF A BAND!

Enslave

Principal Nichols is rambling on. "Nate, this assembly is IMPORTANT! I want our message to be delivered in a MEMORABLE WAY!"

"WHOA! REALLY?" I blurt out. My whole body is tingling. "I mean. . . YEAH! We could do that!"

"Do you honestly think you can compose a song by tomorrow morning?" he asks.

(That's not bragging, by the way. It took me less than half an hour to write our latest song, "It's a Pen's World, and I'm a #2 Pencil.")

"You don't have to make up a song from NOTHING," Principal Nichols says.

Well, it's not exactly Top 40 material. But Enslave the Mollusk can make it rock. I'll just get the guys together after school, and. . .

Principal Nichols raises an eyebrow. "Is there a problem?"

"Um. . . sort of," I tell him.

"Hmmm." Principal Nichols rubs his chin, then drops his voice to a whisper. "Then I suppose you leave me no choice, Nate."

TO GIVE YOU ENOUGH TIME TO WORK ON YOUR **SONG**...

...I'LL HAVE TO **CANCEL** YOUR **DETENTION!**

I can hardly believe what I'm hearing. "You WILL? And Chad's, too?"

"That depends," he says with a smile. "Is Chad in the band?"

"Umm. . . well, not quite," I admit. "But he's sort of like our unofficial manager."

CHAD FACT:
He plays the oboe, but the only song he knows is "Three Blind Mice."

SKWEEONK!! EEEE ONK OONK HONK OOT! BLURK

"All right, BOTH you and Chad are off the hook. . ."
Then he remembers who he is and wags a finger
at me. " . . .JUST THIS ONCE!"

...AND NATE, I'M EXPECTING AN **A PLUS** PERFORMANCE FROM ENSLAVE THE MOLLUSK TOMORROW!

COUNT ON IT!

I peel out of there before he changes his mind.
Wow, this is CRAZY. Wait till I tell the guys our
band is going to rock the assembly tomorrow –
in front of the whole school!

...AND WAIT 'TIL I TELL CHAD HIS **DETENTION** WAS CANCELLED!

THAT **NEVER** HAPPENS!

But this is weird: When I DO tell Chad – during gym class – he doesn't seem surprised at all.

Huh? "Your lucky RABBIT'S foot, you mean?"

He shakes his head, then pulls something from his pocket. "Nope. It's just a foot, see?"

Uh. . . OK. I don't want to sound mean, but that's just some grubby piece of moulded plastic.

"What makes you think it's lucky?" I ask.

For the second time today, Chad blushes like his butt's on fire. "Well. . . as soon as I picked it up. . ."

...MAYA CAME BY!

...AND GUESS WHAT? SHE ACTUALLY **TALKED** TO ME!

I THOUGHT SHE BARELY KNEW MY **NAME**! NOW SHE MIGHT BE STARTING TO **LIKE** ME!

THAT **PROVES** MY LUCKY FOOT WORKS!

No it doesn't, Romeo. Look, I'm glad that Chad and Maya are on their way to Happy Town, but that little plastic foot has nothing to do with it.

REAL good luck charms are RARE.

YOU CAN'T JUST **MAKE** ONE BY PULLING THE LEGS OFF A **G.I. JOE!**

But I've forgotten all about that by 3:15, when all four members of Enslave the Mollusk meet in my garage. And we are STOKED.

"Nate," Artur asks, "where is Fitness Zone paper from Principal Nichols?"

Francis, Teddy, and I loosen up with one of our best songs: "Why Do They Call It Hot Lunch When My Meat Loaf Is So Cold?" It sounds OK, but. . .

The three of us step outside, and. . . hey, what's THIS? He's halfway up the block!

"I am not feel so much like rocking," he mumbles. He's got a look on his face I've never seen before.

"Artur," I say, a little ticked off. "We're wasting time. What's your problem?"

Note to self: Next time you make a list of stupid

pet names for Artur, DESTROY THE EVIDENCE!

I jam the list into my pocket. "This is nothing, Artur," I tell him. "It's a JOKE, that's all."

"Yes. So funny," he says. "Except for nobody is laughing." He turns on his heel and walks off.

"Wait!" Francis calls after him. "What about Enslave the Mollusk?"

CHAPTER 5

Nice move, Artur. Way to bail on us the day before our big debut. Yeah, maybe the list was a little snarky, but. . .

Francis scans the piece of paper that just cost us our lead singer. "I'd be sensitive, TOO. . . ," he says,

"But we ALL do that!" I protest. "The three of us call each other names ALL THE TIME!"

Francis nods. "I guess that's true. . ."

"You're BOTH dipwads," Teddy says. "You're standing around ARGUING. . ."

He's right. We head back into the garage. I guess I should be researching my War of 1812 report, but why waste your brain cells on the Battle of Buttswab when you can write a classic rock anthem called. . .

We all agree that I'll do the singing. Francis and Teddy both have "issues" in that department.

FRANCIS ISSUE:	TEDDY ISSUE:
His voice has been declared a natural disaster.	He can't sing and play at the same time.

OOOWOOOH... FOLLOW YOUR DREEEEAM...

How 'bout we start with "Chopsticks"?

PLINK PLONK

Hours later, we finally call it a night. "Think we're ready?" Francis asks.

"Oh, we're ready," I answer.

READY TO BLOW THE SCHOOL'S **ROOF** OFF!

TOMORROW THE LEGEND OF ENSLAVE THE MOLLUSK **BEGINS**!!

I never thought our big break would be singing about diet and exercise in the cafetorium. And I figured that when we got famous, Artur would be right there with us. I feel sort of bad about that. But I can't worry about it now.

Yeah, I know – there probably won't be any talent scouts roaming the hallways of P.S. 38. . .

Assemblies are always at the start of the day. So the next morning, we need to set up our gear first thing. We're on our way to the cafetorium when we walk right into The Marcus Show.

That's Marcus Goode. He's a seventh grader, and he's way cool. I'm not sure why. But if Marcus gives you his seal of approval, it's like winning the lottery. (At least that's what I've heard. He doesn't talk to sixth graders.)

MARCUS FACT: He started wearing vintage hockey jerseys to school, and now EVERYONE's doing it.

HEY, YOU!

Whoa, does he mean US? I didn't think Marcus even knew we were ALIVE.

"Uh. . . yeah! Yeah, we are," I tell him.

He gives me an approving nod. "That's cool," he says. "Maybe for once the assembly won't be a total dweeb-a-thon."

Francis laughs like a cat coughing up a hairball, but Marcus doesn't seem to notice.

"Did you hear that?" Teddy whispers excitedly. "He DUDED us!"

"And he FIST-BUMPED me!" I add. "That's GOLD!"

Plus, it looks like my slump is officially OVER. I was already pretty sure about that. Now, with the thumbs-up from Marcus, aka Joe Popular. . .

Ah! JENNY! Maybe she wants to wish me good luck before the show.

WHAT'S WRONG WITH **ARTUR**?

Or maybe not.

"He told me he quit the band, but he won't say WHY," she tells me. "What HAPPENED?"

Wow. I guess Artur didn't tell Jenny about the list. My stomach tightens. I wish I'd never made that stinkin' thing. How am I supposed to explain why he quit without looking like a jerk?

WILL YOU ASK HIM WHY HE'S SO **SAD**? HE'LL TALK TO YOU!

HE **TRUSTS** YOU!

Ouch. Hello, guilt trip. First stop: Shame City.

Finally I mumble, "Yeah, I. . . uh. . . I can talk to him."

Huh. She DID end up wishing me luck. So how come I feel lower than a snake in a sewer pipe?

Somehow I'm not quite as pumped for the assembly any more. But the show must go on. As kids file into the cafetorium, we set up our gear. Principal Nichols steps to the mike.

At first, I'm just psyched that he actually got our NAME right. Then, as the applause erupts from the crowd, my skin starts to tingle. The whole school – teachers, students, EVERYBODY – is here. This is it. THIS IS OUR BIG MOMENT!

Francis hits his opening chord, and Teddy plays the intro. Then they both turn to me. I open my mouth and. . .

Nothing. I mean, ZIP.

I'm TRYING. But I can't. My mouth feels full of sawdust. My heart is pounding through my ribs. And my brain? Totally missing in action.

BUT MY VOICE **STINKS!**

IT'S THE ONLY VOICE WE'VE GOT! **HIT IT!**

HAVE YOU EVER CLIMBED SOME STAIRS
AND SAID "WOW, THAT'S EXHAUSTING"?
HAVE YOU EVER SPENT A DAY
JUST EATING CHOCOLATE FROSTING?

DO YOU EVER WATCH TV
UNTIL YOU'RE IN A TRANCE?
ARE YOU HAVING DIFFICULTIES
FITTING IN YOUR PANTS?

OOOH, TIME TO CHANGE YOUR WAYS,
AND YOU DON'T HAVE TO DO IT ALONE!
OOOH, HELLO, HEALTHY DAYS!
STARTING NOW, OUR SCHOOL'S A

FITNESS ZONE !!

TWONG! TAP PLONK

Francis sings a couple more verses about eating broccoli and getting exercise, but I barely hear them. I'm not even paying attention to my drumming. I'm just trying not to throw up.

There's a smattering of polite applause. And if you've ever been in a rock band, you know that polite applause is like kissing your sister. We slink off the stage and into the hallway.

The cafetorium doors swing open, an ocean of kids pours out. . . and look who's leading the pack: Marcus.

He stops right in front of us, and so does everyone else. You can tell they're all waiting to hear what he says about the worst five minutes of our lives.

That makes it official: We're a joke. As we shuffle off to class, Francis and Teddy get their share of grief, but most of the teasing is aimed straight at me. After all, I'M the one who practically wet my pants up there.

The day seems like it'll never end. If I get asked even one more time where my mute button is, someone's going to get a drumstick up their nose. Then the bell rings. FINALLY.

Ladies and gentlemen, Enslave the Mollusk has left the building.

CHAPTER 6

It's a week later, and everybody's STILL picking on me about the assembly. (By the way, T.T. stands for "Tongue-Tied." Hilarious, right?)

"Don't listen to them, Nate," Dee Dee says over a lunch of – I'm not kidding – tofu burgers and three-bean goulash. "PLENTY of people have blanked out on stage! Even ME!"

DURING MY THIRD-GRADE PRODUCTION OF "ALICE IN WONDERLAND," I FORGOT **ALL MY LINES!**

I JUST **STOOD** THERE SAYING **NOTHING!**

Wow. Dee Dee saying nothing. What a concept.

I know she's only trying to make me feel better. But it's not just my Hall of Shame moment at the assembly that's bugging me.

YAK YAK YAK YAK YAK YAK YAK YAK YAK YAK YAK YAK YAK YAK YAK YAK YAK YAK YAK YAK YAK YAK YAK YAK YAK YAK YAK YAK YAK YAK YAK YAK YAK YAK YAK YAK YAK YAK YAK YAK YAK YAK YAK YAK YAK YAK YAK YAK YAK YAK YAK YAK YAK YAK YAK YAK

IT'S WHAT HAPPENED **AFTER** THAT!

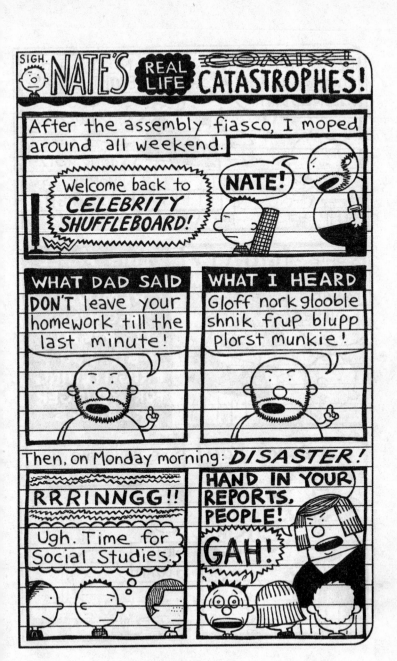

That's Parenting 101: Your kid brings home a pretty solid report card – except for social studies, it was all B's, plus an A in art – but do you say anything about THOSE grades? Nope. Why ruin a perfectly good meltdown with some PRAISE?

Dad was so mad, he didn't even punish me right away. He said he needed time to come up with an "appropriate response." Translation: He wants to watch me SQUIRM for a while.

I've never had a D before, so I'll bet Dad comes down pretty hard. But what'll he do? Pull me off the soccer team? Tell me I have to quit the Doodlers? Make me eat egg salad every day for the rest of my. . .

THUNK THUNK
THUNK THUNK
THUNK THUNK
THUNK THUNK

Looks like Marcus has started another trend. The hockey shirt is history. Now he's rocking a basketball jersey. And so are all his groupies.

"What's with the bottle, champ?" he asks. And for the record, that "champ" didn't sound too friendly.

Marcus rubs his chin. "Makes sense," he says to all the suck-ups surrounding him. "Don't you think so, guys?"

"Yeah," Marcus continues. "It TOTALLY makes sense. . ."

My cheeks burn as Marcus and the Marcettes stroll off, their laughter echoing in my ears. What a. . .

"Jerk," Dee Dee mutters as we get up from the table. "Why's he picking on YOU?"

"I don't know about the target on your back," Dee Dee tells me.

Great. I've got a TAIL. There's enough gum here to stretch all the way to Alaska. Which is where I wish I were right now. ANYWHERE but here.

We scoot out of the cafetorium as fast as we can

and run right into Francis and Teddy.

"Nothing," I grumble. "Just another train wreck."

"Uh, speaking of trains. . . ," Francis says.

Chad fishes something out of his pocket and hands it to me.

It's the little plastic foot Chad found last week.

"Your good luck charm?"

Chad nods. "YOUR luck's in the toilet, right?"

I roll my eyes. "You could say that."

"Then TAKE it!" he tells me. "It's been working great for ME!"

Yeah, I remember what I said last week – that this probably isn't a REAL good luck charm. But the way things are going. . .

We all like gym – but only when Coach CALHOUN is in charge. On Tuesdays and Thursdays, Coach JOHN takes over. And today's Thursday.

We all hustle into the locker room. As I wait for the guys to finish changing, I tuck Chad's foot into my sock. Hey, why not?

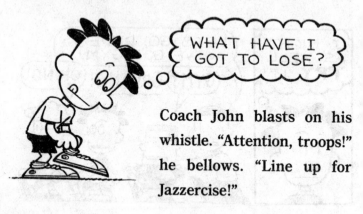

WHAT HAVE I GOT TO LOSE?

Coach John blasts on his whistle. "Attention, troops!" he bellows. "Line up for Jazzercise!"

Ugh. Jazzercise STINKS. We just stand in one spot for half an hour doing cheeseball dance moves. It looks like a group audition for the world's worst music video.

DANCE, BABY, DANCE! SHAKESHAKESHAKE YOUR PANTS! CLONK! *SIGH* DOOF!

"Why can't we play basketball?" someone asks.

BECAUSE I **SAY** SO.

Yeah, and ALSO because if
we play basketball, he's got
to drag his double-wide on to the floor and ref the
game. For Jazzercise, he can crank up his boom
box and spend the class doing crossword puzzles.
Anybody got a five-letter word for "lazy"?

It ticks me off. Why does Coach John always get to
decide what we do? Can't someone ELSE decide?
Can't someone PROTEST? Someone like. . .

Coach John's eyes narrow into slits. "What was that?" he growls.

There's no turning back now. I swallow hard. "The school's a Fitness Zone, right? And basketball's a WAY better workout than Jazzercise."

At first Coach John doesn't say anything. Maybe he's stunned that a student stood up to him. Or maybe he's stealth farting. It's hard to tell.

Finally he grabs a basketball from the rack. "Well, THAT sounds fair!" he says in his fakiest fake voice. "I'll be HAPPY to let you play basketball. . ."

...IF **YOU'LL** DO SOMETHING FOR **ME!**

"Um. . . OK," I answer cautiously. "Like what?"

"Nothing too difficult." He smirks. "All you have to do is make a basket! Just ONE BASKET!"

...FROM **MID-COURT!**

...**BACKWARDS!**

...WITH YOUR **EYES CLOSED!**

BOOMP!

OOF!

"That sounds fair, don't you think?" he asks. Sure. Fair for HIM. This is a sucker bet. Coach John knows he can't lose.

"Now, if you MISS it, you'll be Jazzercising for a MONTH!" he continues, steering me to the centre of the floor. "But I'm SURE you can make it. . ."

...WITH A LITTLE **LUCK!**

Luck. Great. I've had so MUCH of that lately.

A SHOT FROM MID-COURT IS EXACTLY 41 FEET, 9 INCHES!

SSSH!

My palms are sweatier than Coach John's armpits. I glance over at the other kids and notice Chad giving me a thumbs-up. I remember his little plastic foot. If that thing DOES have any luck in it, now's the time to find out. I take one last look at the basket, turn around, close my eyes. . .

. . .and take my best shot.

CHAPTER 7

SHO OFF!

The ball flies right through the hoop like it's remote controlled. It doesn't even graze the rim. It barely touches the NET.

120

The whole gym goes completely bananas, except for two people:

Coach John. . . . . . .and Dee Dee.

Talk about a MIRACLE. For half a second, I think about sticking it right in Coach John's face. . .

. . .but I don't. I'm not insane. Plus, I remember one of Chad's grandmother's goofy sayings:

"DON'T POKE THE BEAR!"

"HE MIGHT **EAT** YOU!"

Or he might make you do squat thrusts until you hurl. Do I really want to taste that three-bean goulash a SECOND time? (Short answer. Starts with "N." Rhymes with "go.")

So I act like sinking a backwards half-court shot with my eyes closed is no biggie. And we spend the next hour – sorry, Dee Dee – actually having FUN.

HUFF PUFF WHEEZE

Later, on the way to maths, Chad nudges me.

I show the foot to the guys. Francis frowns. We all know that look. Here comes one of his Smarty McKnow-It-All comments.

"There's absolutely no proof that so-called good luck charms have ANY effect on real-life events," he announces.

"He might have made that shot WITHOUT the plastic foot," Francis points out. "For me to believe it's REALLY a good luck charm. . ."

We cruise into the maths room and take our seats. Mr Staples waves his arms for quiet. Then. . .

Wait, WHAT? We just had a pop quiz LAST Thursday. Isn't this illegal? Or unconstitutional? Or SOMETHING?

Too bad Francis is out of noogie range. But he could be right: Maybe Chad's foot is just. . . a foot.

"You have thirty minutes to complete the quiz," Mr Staples tells us. "You may beginnn. . . NOW."

Something's screwy here. Where did these maths problems come from, PLUTO? Other kids seem confused, too. Even GINA looks clueless.

"Really?" Mr Staples says in surprise. He turns to the nearest desk. "Mark, may I look at your quiz?"

"I don't mean you, Mark," he adds quickly. (Fact check: Mark actually IS a moron. He's also got a serious earwax issue.)

As he shuts the door behind him, the classroom starts buzzing.

Just so you know: T.S.U.s are Teacher Screw-Ups, and they happen more than you think. After all, teachers are human. Sort of. Whenever a teacher pulls a T.S.U., we kids are all over it.

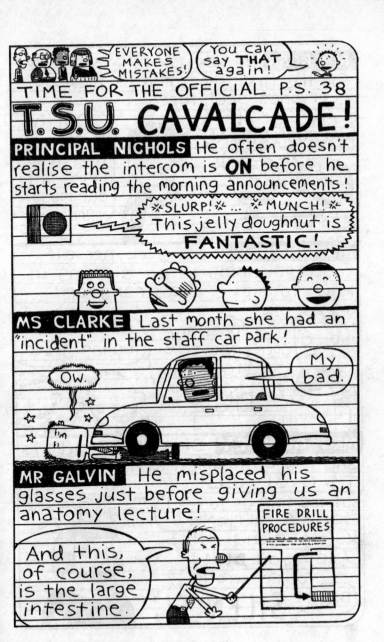

The door swings open. Mr Staples is back, looking a little flustered. "Well," he says, "so much for THAT idea."

So maths is a breeze. And there's more good news in science. Mr Galvin isn't even THERE.

After school, I practically float out of the building. "No maths quiz and no Galvin!" I crow to Francis. "What do you think of Chad's foot NOW?"

"I'm still not convinced," he sniffs. "Yeah, those were lucky breaks, but they were lucky for EVERYONE."

I have no idea who this lady is. But she's sure happy to see ME.

"You WONDERFUL boy!" she gushes. "Where on earth did you FIND it?"

"Right here in the grass," I tell her, handing it over.

She beams at me. "Bless your heart, young man. This necklace is IRREPLACEABLE!"

MY HUSBAND GAVE IT TO ME **FIFTY YEARS AGO!**

"How ROMANTIC!" Dee Dee sighs.

The woman looks so happy, I can't help but feel kind of good that I found her necklace. And then, seconds later, I feel even BETTER.

A GOOD DEED LIKE THIS CALLS FOR A **REWARD!**

MAY I GIVE YOU TWENTY DOLLARS?

"And I won't take no for an answer!" she tells me.

Obviously, she has no idea that saying no to twenty bucks never even crossed my mind.

"Wow!" I stammer. "THANK you!"

"OK, OK. The foot works." Francis chuckles. "I can't argue with twenty dollars."

"Me, neither. Come on, you guys!" I say, waving the bill over my head.

We trade stupid tofu jokes until Dee Dee changes the subject.

As usual, she's as subtle as a sledgehammer.

Chad doesn't answer. He doesn't HAVE to. His cheeks have gone code red.

"I think you should ask her out," Dee Dee continues. "You two would make a cute couple."

"Pump the brakes, Cupid," Teddy says. "He'll ask her when he's good and ready. Right, Chad?"

CHAPTER 8

Chad's not moving. He's frozen in place like a redheaded garden gnome. Then we see why.

138

Marcus and his travelling road show are playing Hacky Sack across the street. All the kids over there are seventh graders. . . except one.

"So did I," Chad mumbles. He looks lower than an ant's ankles.

Chillax, Dee Dee. No need to go into drama queen overdrive. This is CHAD'S tragedy, not yours.

Besides, I know EXACTLY why Maya's cosying up to Marcus: He's a seventh grader. See, girls grow up faster than guys. (We learned that from Coach John in "Health & Hygiene." The lesson that day was "Our Changing Bodies." Awkward.)

Anyway, we found out that your average sixth-grade girl is like the age of a seventh-grade boy, maturity-wise. Which means that all of us sixth-grade guys are at the very bottom of. . .

It doesn't ALWAYS happen like that (Exhibit A: Jenny and Artur), but it's pretty common. Nobody's shocked when a sixth-grade girl likes a seventh-grade boy. Except Chad.

"Chad, wait!" I call out. "I'll buy you a Gut Buster!"

"No, thanks," he answers. "I forgot that. . . uh. . . I told my mum I'd come straight home after school."

I peel out for my house at warp speed. With all the good luck vibes flying around when school ended, I totally forgot about what Dad said when I left the house this morning.

COME **STRAIGHT HOME** AFTER SCHOOL!

WE'LL TALK ABOUT YOUR **REPORT CARD!**

You know what's worse than having an appointment to get yelled at? Being LATE for it.

"Forgotten? Me? No. . ."

Hm. Don't know where he's going with this, but at least he's not pitching a fit. And as long as read-along time doesn't involve one of Ellen's cheeseball novels about vampire supermodels, I'm there.

In all my years of teaching, I have never encountered such an undisciplined student. He is inattentive and often disruptive during class, and he seems more concerned with making jokes than doing his schoolwork.

"Nice. Ol' Dragon Breath's got a real way with words," I grumble.

"Actually, ol' Drag— er, Mrs Godfrey didn't write this. It was written by Mrs Brodie."

My jaw drops into my lap. WHAT??

He smiles. "Tough to imagine me as a sixth grader?"

Tough? Try IMPOSSIBLE. I can't even imagine him with HAIR.

"Nate," Dad says, "I have a confession to make."

I... UH... WASN'T EXACTLY AN HONOUR ROLL STUDENT.

Really? Wow! Maybe we should have these father-son talks more OFTEN!

"It's not that I didn't TRY," he adds quickly. "It was just that sometimes. . . well. . . sometimes. . ."

...STUFF HAPPENED!

RIGHT.

AND I UNDERSTAND THAT STUFF SOMETIMES HAPPENS IN **YOUR** LIFE, TOO.

I roll my eyes. "You can say that again."

(Rats. I knew there was a "but" coming.)

"I'm ALSO not telling you it's OK to get a D in social studies," he says, switching back to "bad cop" mode. "Clearly, you need to spend a lot more time on your homework."

Hey, what's there to argue about? Considering how bad Dad COULD have slammed me . . .

...I GOT OFF PRETTY **EASY**!

At least, that's my FIRST reaction. But a few hours later – after supper (Anyone for "meat loaf jubilee"?), homework (I officially hate whoever invented fractions), and a shower (thanks for using all the hot water, Ellen), I'm starting to realise this will be harder than I thought.

I mean, cartooning is my LIFE. I draw before bed EVERY NIGHT. Without drawing, I can't even SLEEP!

As I toss my trousers into the closet, Chad's lucky foot slips out of the pocket. Whoa. Suddenly, my brain starts connecting the dots.

Dad said I couldn't draw in my NOTEBOOK. He never said I couldn't draw on OTHER stuff! Like

FOOTWEAR, for example. Turns out, a ballpoint pen works GREAT on canvas sneakers. Except an hour later, my size 6's aren't just sneakers any more. They're Nate Wright ORIGINALS!

The next day at school, it's Dee Dee – she's sort of a fashion geek – who notices them first.

And since Dee Dee's voice is louder than a jackhammer on steroids, it's not long before other kids start crowding around.

A girl named Shauna speaks up. "Marcus, look at Nate's SHOES!"

Marcus saunters over. He glances down at my feet and snorts. "Big WOW! He took a pair of cheap sneakers and drew PICTURES on them!"

There's some mumbling as all eyes turn from my feet to his. Then Shauna says quietly, "Yeah, but. . ."

Heads start nodding. More kids push past Marcus to look at my sneakers up close. He shrugs uncertainly, then looks around for his posse.

He shuffles away. But the group of kids that follows him isn't as big as it usually is.

Teddy stares at me wide-eyed after they're gone. "Dude! Do you know what this means?"

YOU'RE COOLER THAN MARCUS!

CHAPTER 9

The Great Sneaker Scribble is on. By lunchtime, half the kids in school have customised their sneakers, just like yours truly.

"Did you hear that?" Francis says as we sit down.

"Personally, I think you're more like an adjective," Teddy cracks. "You know, DESCRIPTIVE words."

He glares at me as he rubs his head. "I thought you said getting hit with a bottle feels GOOD."

"It DOES, Einstein," I tell him. "But it helps if the bottle's EMPTY."

I don't know their names, but I recognise these kids. They're seventh graders. And they're both part of Marcus's posse of wanna-be's.

"Sure," I say. I hand over the bottle.

"Just. . . uh. . . trying out Nate's bottle, Marcus," the kid named Jeremy stammers.

"Well, you look like a MORON," Marcus sneers. "Knock it off."

Marcus looks disgusted. "Fine! You want to copy

some snot-nosed sixth grader?"

BE MY **GUEST!**

C'MON, MAYA.

As Marcus stalks off, Dee Dee sails in. "Can I join the party?" she asks.

...OR DO I NEED A **RESERVATION** TO SIT WITH *JOE COOL?*

WINKA WINKA!

"What's that supposed to mean?" I say.

She rolls her eyes. "Boys are so dense," she sighs. "Look AROUND you!"

"They're imitating you! You're a TRENDSETTER!"

"Yeah, but it's not like I'm TRYING to set trends! It's just. . . well. . . everything is. . . it's. . ."

IT'S THE **GOOD LUCK FOOT!**

NATE CAN DO **NO WRONG!**

Bingo. I haven't said much about the foot because I don't want to jinx it. . . but LOOK at everything that's happened since Chad gave it to me! I sank that miracle shot in gym. Some

160

lady gave me twenty bucks. Dad didn't ground me. And now kids I don't even know are asking:

Bottom line: This is the most epic good luck streak of my life. Maybe of ANYONE'S life. And it just keeps on rolling. I'm officially. . .

"So. . . what are you gonna do today?" Teddy asks as we walk to school the next morning.

Wow. Got sarcasm? He's probably sick of me playing Lucky the Leprechaun 24/7. I can't blame him; I used to feel the same way about. . .

Yup. Artur. So much stuff has gone right for me lately, I'd almost forgotten about our little. . . uh. . . "incident."

"Can I talk to you for a sec?"

There's a pause. "Hokay," he says finally.

Then. . . silence. Suddenly my vocal chords are having a panic attack. I know what I want to say. . . so why can't I spit it out? I stuff my hands in my pockets and feel Chad's plastic foot.

Come on, foot. Help me do this.

"I have no idea why I did it," I tell him. "Well, maybe I SORT of do, but I. . ."

"Nate." Artur holds up his hand. "You do not have

to explaining. I am understand why you did it."

Ouch. Hey, thanks for the honesty, Artur. How about a little LESS of it next time?

"Yes. I know this feelings," he continues.

OK, now THAT'S a surprise. "Uh. . . you do?" I ask, trying to sound casual. "How come?"

Now it's Artur's turn to look surprised. "Is it

not so total OBVIOUS, Nate?" he says.

Wow. I'll admit I'VE always thought my life rocked, but I never knew ARTUR did.

He chuckles. "You are always get in the middle of so crazy happenings."

I groan. "Yeah. Like at the ASSEMBLY."

167

He breaks into a huge smile. I think that's a yes.

"Come on!" I say.

LET'S GO AND TELL FRANCIS AND TEDDY THAT ENSLAVE THE MOLLUSK WILL **ROCK AGAIN!**

WHOA! SLOW DOWN, GENTS!

SAVE THE RUNNING FOR **FIELD DAY!**

"What's Field Day?" I ask.

"Just another part of our Fitness Zone programme," Coach explains. "The whole school's going to take part in a friendly athletic competition!"

"It's not a DANCE-OFF, Twinkle Toes," I tell her. "It's SPORTS. It's a CONTEST."

"Well, I happen to like activities that aren't all INTENSE," she sniffs. "There are no winners or losers in Jazzercise!"

"You're half right," I crack.

"Dee Dee has a point, Nate," Coach says.

"See? He AGREED with me," Dee Dee says as Coach walks off. "It doesn't MATTER who comes in first!"

Uh-oh. Here comes trouble.

"The seventh grade is going to DEMOLISH the sixth grade on Field Day!" Marcus crows.

"Yes, I am agree," Artur says matter-of-factly. "Because you are a whole year more OLDER."

Marcus smirks. "No, because sixth graders are totally LAME."

"Why are you BETTING?" Dee Dee chirps. "Coach said it's not about who wins, it's about FITNESS!"

"He was right," Marcus says with a snort. "You sixth graders could USE a little fitness!"

"Hey, superchunk, come over here!" Marcus calls.

Chad edges slowly towards us. "M-me?" he asks.

Chad's cheeks turn pink. "That's not my name.
My name's Chad."

Marcus isn't impressed. "OK. CHAD. . ."

"You leave him alone," Dee Dee growls.

Marcus holds up his hands in mock innocence.
"Hey, I'm just having a friendly conversation with
CHAD here! And besides. . ."

CHAPTER 10

Marcus looks stunned. We ALL do. Nobody's ever heard Maya raise her voice. But, hey, there's a first time for everything.

"OK, OK!" Marcus mumbles. "You don't have to throw a FIT about it."

Maya jerks her hand away. "Why would you want ME tagging along?" she says angrily.

"Not YOU!" Marcus tells her. He waves a hand at the rest of us. "I was talking about THESE losers!"

"They're NOT lame, and they're NOT losers!" Maya says, her voice shaking. "They're my FRIENDS!"

Marcus nods. "Isn't that sweet."

YOU CAN ALL BE PATHETIC **TOGETHER!**

"What a slimeball," I mutter. Maya looks like she might start bawling. Then. . .

CHAD, I... I'M...

? ?

SNIFF!

"OK, it's official," I say. "I don't understand girls."

Dee Dee rolls her eyes. "On behalf of girls everywhere, thanks for the news flash."

Dee Dee gives me one of her you're-as-dumb-as-a-sock-puppet head shakes. "Why do you THINK?"

"Well, what would YOU call him? She obviously LIKES the guy!"

"Maya doesn't like Marcus," Dee Dee declares, almost poking my eye out as she waves her finger.

"Then why have she and Marcus been superglued together for the past week?" I ask.

"What I MEANT was, put yourself in Maya's shoes," Dee Dee explains. "She's SHY! She's QUIET! When Mr Seventh Grade Big Shot started paying attention to her..."

...SHE WAS PROBABLY **FLATTERED**!

BUT NOW SHE'S SEEN MARCUS BEING A **JERK**! SHE'S EMBARRASSED! SHE'S **MORTIFIED**!!

HOW YOU CAN BE SURE?

Dee Dee strikes a pose. "Ahem..." she says.

WE WOMEN JUST **KNOW** THESE THINGS!

OH, BROTHER.

CHAD, WHY DON'T **YOU** GO AND TALK TO MAYA?

He blushes. "But. . . what would I say?"

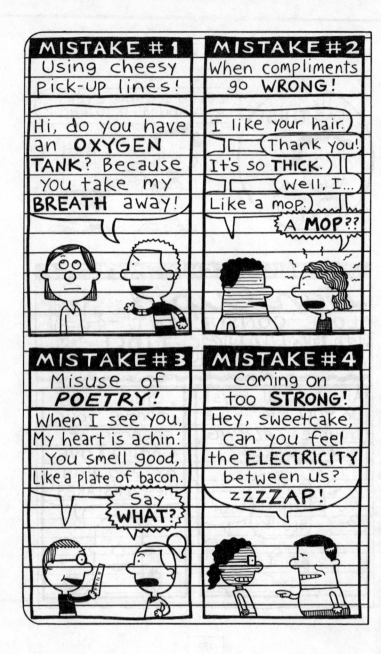

Chad hands the comic back to me. "I don't think this'll do me much good," he sighs.

"Just do whatever you did LAST time," I tell him. "The two of you had a long talk in the cafetorium, didn't you?"

"Yeah," Chad says. "But that was. . . before."

"Before what?" Dee Dee asks, but Chad doesn't have time to say anything. I've already pulled the answer out of my pocket.

"I hope you're right," Chad says quietly. "Thanks, Nate. You're a real friend."

HONNNNK!

"Oh, don't mind me," Dee Dee sniffs, wiping glop off her nose. "I get emotional sometimes."

I try to keep a straight face. "YOU? No way."

The bell interrupts Dee Dee's drama-rama. "Better stick a cork in it," I tell her. "We've got home room."

NATE. I HAVE QUESTION FOR YOU.

SINCE YOU GIVE AWAY LUCKY FOOT TO CHAD, WHAT IF **YOUR** LIFE NOW TURNS TO DISASTER?

"I'm hoping that won't happen," I answer.

Or maybe not. Someone must have crawled out from under the wrong side of the rock this morning.

"Before the bell rang, young man," Mrs Godfrey hisses at me through clenched teeth. . .

I DID A **DESK INSPECTION!**

Uh-oh. That means she's not just trolling for desktop graffiti. She's sticking her big fat nose INSIDE our desks, too. Which, in case you were wondering, is bad news for me.

EXPLAIN it? OK. It's a work of cartooning genius.
Need I say more?

"'Ultra-Nate and Mega-Chad,'" she reads aloud, at about one syllable per second. "Obviously, this drawing was a TEAM EFFORT!"

Poor Chad looks like a minnow in a shark tank. "Wait," I protest. "Chad didn't have anything to do with this."

Mrs Godfrey stares me down. "I'll determine that for myself, if you don't mind."

"N-no, ma'am," Chad squeaks.

Her eyes narrow. "What's that in your hand?"

THIS? UM... JUST A... A GOOD LUCK CHARM.

"It looks like part of a TOY," she says. "And toys are not permitted in this classroom. Hand it over."

Mrs Godfrey drops the foot into her desk drawer. Then she gets back to business. "Chad, you may return to your seat."

...AND NATE...

YOU MAY REPORT TO DETENTION AFTER SCHOOL!

RRIP!

Gee, THAT went well. I flop down into my chair and sneak a glance over at Chad. He's staring miserably into space. I know how he feels. Looks like the good luck streak is officially over. . .

CHAPTER 11

I spend the next four days praying for rain, but it's no use. On the morning of Field Day, there's not a cloud in the sky.

"We just saw you talking to MARCUS!" Francis says. "How come?"

I grimace. "We were finalising our bet."

BUT YOU MADE THAT BET WHEN YOU STILL HAD THE **LUCKY FOOT**!

WHY DIDN'T YOU CALL IT OFF?

I shake my head. "I can't back out. That would make me a bigger weasel than HE is."

"Like that's possible," Teddy grumbles.

ALL I CAN DO IS HOPE THAT SOMEHOW THE SIXTH GRADE CAN FIND A WAY TO WIN **ONE EVENT**!

Welcome to **FIELD DAY**!

"It COULD happen," Francis says, not very convincingly.

"Captains?" I say in surprise. "Who's our captain?"

Teddy shrugs. "Beats me."

"SOMEBODY needed to take charge," she smirks as she tapes a sheet of paper to the flagpole. "I've taken the liberty of creating an official event schedule."

"Mark Cheswick running the hundred-metre dash?" I say. "Anne Marie Abruzzi throwing the shot put?"

Gina folds her arms. "Yes. So?"

I look around and lower my voice. "They'll get DESTROYED!" I hiss. "At least put people in events they could actually WIN!"

"The whole point of Field Day is FITNESS, dork face!" she snarls. "I'm not TRYING to win!"

"Huh? Oh. . . uh. . . no, Coach."

"Good. Because being part of a TEAM. . ."

...MEANS **RESPECTING** YOUR **CAPTAIN!**

Even when she's Captain CLUELESS? Gina grins in triumph and flounces off. My event's not till later. For now, there's nothing to do. . .

Want to hear the sad part? Those were some of our BETTER events. Obviously, if I want to win this bet with Marcus. . .

Coach's voice echoes across the field. "The next event is the SIXTY-METRE HURDLES!"

Yikes, that kid's legs come up to my NECK. He looks like he can STEP over the hurdles. I probably don't have much of a chance. But. . .

And then. . . something DOES happen. Kareem trips! As he scrambles to his feet, I'm already clearing the first hurdle.

I'm really moving now. Four hurdles to go. I peek to my left. Kareem's gaining fast, but he's going to run out of room. Three hurdles to go. Two. . .

It's like one of those slow-motion nightmares. As the blood rushes through my head and I try to get back up, I hear Kareem's footsteps pound by me.

And here comes the welcoming committee.

Dee Dee zips over and starts brushing the dirt and grass off me. "No snappy comeback?" she asks.

"What's there to say?" I mutter.

"Yeah. Which we have zero chance of winning."

Dee Dee frowns. "You look miserable," she tells me. "I don't know who's feeling worse. . ."

YOU OR **CHAD!**

"Poor guy," I say. "So he still hasn't talked to Maya?"

Dee Dee shakes her head. "He says he can't do it without his lucky foot. It's so TRAGIC!"

THEY'D MAKE SUCH A GREAT **TEAM!**

Her words hit me right in the face. "TEAM!" I shout. "Dee Dee! I just thought of something!"

"Where are you going?" she calls as I go sprinting

away. But there's no time to explain. I have to find. . . Ah-HA!

Wondering what I'm up to? Sorry, it's top secret. And if I do say so myself, it's brilliant.

I just hope it works.

FOR THE SEVENTH GRADE, THE CONTESTANTS ARE **MARCUS** AND **JAKOB**!

"And the sixth-grade team is MAYA AND ARTUR!"

Artur leans into me. "Now?" he whispers.

I nod. "Now."

"Excuse, please." Artur hops over to Coach like a frog with arthritis.

I CANNOT DO RACING, BECAUSE I AM HURT MY ANKLE.

WAIT, **WHAT**?

HOP! HOP!

"Artur, you should have reported this injury to me the minute it happened!" Gina huffs. "As captain, it's my job to find an appropriate substitute to take your place in the—"

"Fine," Coach says. "It'll be Maya and Chad, then. Nate, help them get ready, please."

Chad's cheeks are as red as a Christmas stocking. "I've... um... never been in a three-legged race," he says to Maya. "I'll probably be terrible."

She smiles shyly. "I think you'll be great."

Marcus interrupts me. "Hey, dweebus maximus! This is your last chance to win our bet!"

I give him an icy stare. "Yup."

"I picked the fastest runner in the whole school for my partner!" he crows.

"What a great strategy," I say.

For just an instant, his grin falters. Then Coach whistles sharply. "All right, teams, LINE UP!"

ONE! TWO! ONE! TWO! ONE! TWO!

Maya and Chad burst off the line and gradually pick up speed. The seventh graders? Not so much.

WHAT ARE YOU **DOING**? YOU'RE GOING TOO **FAST**!

NO, **YOU'RE** GOING TOO **SLOW**!

"Look at Marcus and Jakob!" Francis exclaims. "They're all herky-jerky!"

Teddy chuckles. "The key word being 'jerky.'"

"Maya and Chad look FABULOUS!" Dee Dee chirps.

"This is fascinating!" Francis says in his nerdiest Nutty Professor voice. "INDIVIDUALLY, they're much slower than the seventh graders. . ."

"What do you think of Marcus and Jakob's teamwork?" Teddy cracks.

"We have expression for this in my country," Artur says. "Is called 'hot mess.'"

The race is over way before Maya and Chad cruise across the finish line. That was more than a win. It was a good old-fashioned butt kicking. I turn to Dee Dee. "You were right about those two," I say.

THEY **DO** MAKE A GREAT TEAM!

"OK, guys," I say. "When Principal Nichols introduces us. . ."

"Only the MELODY is the same, you idiots," I tell them. "The WORDS are different!"

RIGHT, ARTUR?

YES, ABSOLUTENESS!

WINK!

From behind the curtain, we can hear the cafetorium filling up. It's our weekly assembly, and we've got another chance. To ROCK.

"I want to know more about your bet with Marcus," Francis says. "What if you'd LOST?"

"It would have been a nightmare," I answer. "I was going to become a mini-Marcus."

I PROMISED TO DRESS LIKE HIM, ACT LIKE HIM, AND FOLLOW HIM AROUND FOR A WHOLE **WEEK**!

UGH.

"But you WON," Teddy says. "So what does Marcus have to do for YOU?"

Just then Principal Nichols's voice comes blasting over the intercom. "Let's all give a warm P.S. 38 welcome to. . . ENSLAVE THE MOLLUSK!!"

"You're about to find out," I say as the curtain rises. "Hit it, Artur."

THEY SIMPLY COULDN'T UNDERSTAND
THAT **TEAMWORK** MATTERED MOST!
AND THAT IS WHY, AT RACE'S END,
THE SEVENTH GRADE WAS **TOAST**!

OOOOH, THEY WERE STRESSED TO THE MAX,
'CAUSE LOSING TO YOUR RIVAL ISN'T FUN!
OOOOH, THEY SHOULD TRY TO RELAX...

NOW WATCH
WHILE CHAD
SHOWS MARCUS
HOW IT'S DONE!

THUNK THUNK THUNK
THUNK THUNK THUNK
THUNK THUNK
THUNK THUNK
THUNK THUNK
THUNK THUNK
THUNK THUNK
THUNK THUNK...

"Hm. That's odd," Francis chuckles as Chad continues with his. . . uh. . . drum solo.

Artur smiles. "I am feel happy for Chad. He won the race and also gots together with Maya!"

"And he did it all without his good luck foot!" Francis points out.

"We'll never see that foot again," Teddy sighs.

"We're doing OK without it," I remind him.
"Besides, why do we need a foot. . . ."

LIVIN' LARGE!

P.S. 38 is pretty small. Everyone knows everyone else. So whenever a new kid shows up, it's a major event. Especially when he's got a name like **THIS**:

Boys and girls, this is Breckenridge Puffington III!

Anyway, Principal Nichols asked me to be the kid's "buddy," so it's my job to help him make friends...

MOVE it, Puff-ball!

SHOVE!

...and to show him around the school, which is falling apart. That's what happens when a building is one hundred years old.

CLONK!

OW!